Man-nerisms

How to Effectively Respect Your Man

Shawn McBride

Mannerisms

Copyright © 2021 by Shawn McBride

All rights reserved. No part of this book may be reproduced or transmitted in any form or by any means without written permission from the author.

ISBN: 9798638944186

Table of Contents

Introduction: R.E.S.P.E.C.T 8

Chapter 1: Respect Says: "I Admire You" 13

Chapter 2: Respect Says: "I Appreciate You" 21

Chapter 3: Respect Says: "I Submit To Your Authority & Leadership" 31

Chapter 4: Respect Says: "I Will Show You Sexual Attention" 37

Chapter 5: Respect Says: "I Am Available to Play With You" 43

Chapter 6: Respect Says: "I will Keep Myself Attractive for You" 48

Chapter 7: Respect Says: "I Will Attend to Your Domestic Needs" 55

Chapter 8: Respect Says: "I Will Articulate Your Love Language" 61

Conclusion: You Make Him Better! 65

Dedication

Firstly, I dedicate this project to my wife, Dana Michelle McBride, who has been the true model of effectively showing R.E.S.P.E.C.T to me as a man. You have always accepted me for me and supported my hustle, drive, and ambition. You are and always will be my perfect wife and mother to our children.

Also, I would like to dedicate this project to the hundreds of dating, engaged, and married couples I have been privileged to serve over the last two decades. Upon graduation from the seminary in 2001 with my Masters in Counseling, I never could have imagined, in my wildest dreams, the sheer number of couples that I would meet and serve as a pastoral and professional counselor. You have taught me. You have trained me. You have been my teachers and my classroom instructors. I am still learning from each and every one of you.

Thank you for entrusting me with your personal stories.

Disclaimer

These are fictional stories to illustrate what happens in real-life relationships. All names have been changed not to reflect any couple I have personally provided counseling services for over the past two decades.

Introduction

R.E.S.P.E.C.T Otis & Aretha

The song R.E.S.P.E.C.T was sung beautifully by the Queen of Soul and music legend, Aretha Franklin, but did you know that a man wrote the original song? His name was Otis Redding. He released the song in 1965, but just two short years later, in 1967 specifically, it became a hit and signature song for Aretha Franklin. Aretha and her team completely reimagined the song and added their own twists and tunes to it. As it turns out, the original song was not intended to become an anthem for women; rather, it was intended to be a plea from a hard-working man. In Redding's version, the lyrics were a clarion call to his lady. He promised to afford her whatever she wanted and was never concerned about her doing him wrong, as long as he received the due R.E.S.P.E.C.T when he got home.

Ephesians 5:33 (NIV) Each one of you must also love his wife as he loves himself, and the wife must respect her husband.

According to the Holy Scriptures, a wife (woman) needs L.O.V.E from her husband (her man). A husband (man) wants and needs something completely different — he desires R.E.S.P.E.C.T

A woman has one driving need - to feel loved. When that need is met, she is happy. A man has one driving need - to feel respected. When that need is met, he is happy. When either of these needs isn't met, there is relationship madness.

Over the last two decades of working with couples who are dating, engaged, or married, I have discovered that the greatest desire for a woman is to receive LOVE, but a man's greatest desire is to get R.E.S.P.E.C.T. The challenge that I see with couples is that it is hard for a woman to fully respect a man she feels does not properly love her. On the other hand, it is similarly hard for a man to fully love a woman he doesn't feel properly respects him.

To put it differently, when a woman feels unloved by her man, her natural tendency is to act in disrespectful ways toward him. On the flip side, when a man feels disrespected by his lady, his natural tendency is to act in unloving ways toward her. Let me break it down further. Without LOVE, she reacts without respect. Without respect, he reacts without love.

If couples can grasp these fundamental concepts and begin to live out its implications, their relationship, in my opinion, can begin to thrive and not just survive.

For the sake of this book's project, MAN-nerisms, I wish to focus on, break down, teach and help women understand specifically what R.E.S.P.E.C.T looks like. In my companion book, *Lady's First*, I will teach a man how to love his lady effectively.

According to a dictionary definition, the word manners are the way of doing something or behaving. The focus of this book is how do you show R.E.S.P.E.C.T to your man and behave toward him?

This concept of R.E.S.P.E.C.T toward a man by his wife is held in the story of Sarah and Abraham, in which Sarah referred to him as lord, a sign of sincere respect. We also know that Sarah, for her unalloyed R.E.S.P.E.C.T for her husband, was rewarded with her dearest wish of a child at ninety. God will reward and show pleasure for your R.E.S.P.E.C.T for your man and execute His wise plan in your relationship.

Chapter 1

Respect Says
I Admire You for Who You Are

"Cheerleader" was a popular song released in 2014 and recorded by Jamaican singer/songwriter Omi whose real name is Omar Samuel Pasley. In the United States sports world, cheerleaders are typically a team of happy, energetic, and athletic females who perform organized cheering, chanting, and dancing to support a sports team at a match.

Their encouragement can breathe life into the team.

In this particular song, O.M.I. sings of having found the right girl, whom he describes as a "cheerleader." From his point of view, she's always there to support him and cheer him on. She admires him! She encourages him! She praises him! She roots and cheers for him.

> *Lyrics: When I need motivation*
> *My one solution is my queen*
> *'Cause she stays strong (yeah yeah)*
> *She is always in my corner*
> *Right there when I want her*
> *All these other girls are tempting*
> *But I'm empty when you're gone*

Admiration means that you are your man's biggest cheerleader!

Short Story for Consideration

Bob is admired by his co-worker, Sandy. Bob eventually has an affair with Sandy. Bob's home was no longer a safe haven. He barely wanted to go home at night. Bob was constantly nagged and attacked by his wife, Barbara. Bob's home was not a place where he felt valued and appreciated. Bob went to a person where he was celebrated and appreciated, not just tolerated.

Admiration[1]

Everyone needs a voice that is a constant encourager to them, a personal private cheerleader. Some teams have never won a game, but if they have someone willing to praise them just for suiting up and playing the game, it breathes life into them.

Cheerleaders don't cheer at games because they are guaranteed a win. A cheerleader cheers because her team is in the game.

Your husband needs a wife who will cheer him on just because he is in the game. As his cheerleader, you are on the field with him, boosting him up when he thinks he cannot go on.

When I was in school, we didn't have the best of teams. Money was low in our school district, and we didn't have the support or foundation that made us an A-1 team. Despite those dismal facts, week after week, our players suited up and played the game.

There were times when they played so hard and would lose by a few points. There were other times when you could tell they were beaten before they hit the field. But there were the occasional victories, some of which were even said to be impossible.

Admiring your man means you notice his manliness, his manly qualities, masculine skills, abilities, achievements, ideas, dreams, and manly body. Simply put, what makes him a man!

Nikki Minaj tells Rick Ross in a popular song these powerful words: "You the boss - You, you, you the boss man." BINGO! This is precisely what your man needs to hear! You see, men want to be admired and feel respected! Never let another female praise your man more than you!

All men have a deep longing to be admired. This has been part of their core structure since they were little boys. He wants you to notice his manly qualities and love him; in turn, when you express admiration for it, he feels admired.

Your man wants you to notice him. If you don't notice his manliness and admire him, another woman will.

What to Admire In Your Man

He wants you to admire his qualities that can only be found in a man. He may appreciate you noticing how kind, thoughtful and handsome he is, but you will do little to stir up his feelings for you with those observations. What he needs to be noticed for are his manly body, skills, achievements, and dreams.

When you notice these traits, you wake up his tender feelings of love and affection for you.

1. *His body* – Notice his physical features. Maybe he's not in the best of shape. You don't have to dwell on that. Find other features that set him apart for you. His strong arms. His height. How his stature makes you feel protected. His strength. Large hands. Beard. Deep voice. Heavy walk.

2. *Masculine Skills and Abilities* – Acknowledge his skills and abilities in his job. Most likely, he has a job, whether in corporate America or manual labor, meant for a man.

3. *Masculine Achievements* – Admire and honor him for advancement at his job. For winning a championship, or in a hobby he enjoys. For outstanding service or completing a difficult task in a masculine field.

4. *Masculine Goals and Dreams* – If he has dreams and goals that he has not yet accomplished in a masculine field, praise him for that. Going after what he desires is hard work. He believes that not just anyone can accomplish those goals.

5. *Masculine Traits and Character* – Is he decisive, steadfast, and aggressive (not in a bad way, but get-things-done-kinda-way)? Let him know you notice. If you have a man that holds the door open for you or your children or any other chivalrous task, give him credit.

6. *Masculine Role* – Not all men fall into this category. I find that it's usually because a strong wife hasn't allowed him to play his part yet. I can say this because this was me! I wore the pants. I said what goes. I controlled the finances. I was in charge. I can tell you; I didn't play a man's role very well. I was stressed and depressed all the time. I screwed up so much, including our relationship.

Let him take over the task of guiding the family. He needs to be the protector and provider. He was created for that. And, when you learn to let him lead, you will love your husband in this role. You can love being taken care of. It feels tremendously special to know that someone else cares so much for you and can do anything for you.

How to Discover Things to Admire

- ✓ Think about him
- ✓ Observe him
- ✓ Listen to him talk

How to Express Admiration Toward Your Man

1. *Be sincere* – Sincerity is essential when you relate to a man's most sensitive nature — pride in himself and his masculinity. He will notice superficial made-up flattery, and it won't be good. It will almost seem like you are trying to make fun of him and his qualities as a man. He may think you are trying to manipulate him, and he will resent you for that.

2. *Suppose you don't yet admire him.* Study and think about him until you can find qualities to admire sincerely.

3. *Be specific* – When admiring your husband, be specific with your praise. Don't just say I love how manly you are, but specify what it is about his manliness you love. For example, "I love seeing your muscles flex when you lift that heavy box for me," or, "I appreciate all that hard yard work you did for me. It takes more strength, like yours, than I have to do that."

Rules for Admiring Your Man

- ✓ Accept him as he is
- ✓ Think about him
- ✓ Observe him
- ✓ Listen to him talk
- ✓ Express admiration in words
- ✓ Be sincere
- ✓ Be specific

HOMEWORK

1. Think about your man. What are the first three words that come to mind?

2. Observe your man today. What are the few things you noticed that you admired?

3. Listen to your man talk. What did he say that made you admire him or feel loved?

Chapter 2

Respect Says
I Appreciate You for What You Do

In an episode of *The Simpsons*, the wayward and rebellious son, Bart Simpson, was given a piece of fruit by his mother. It was an orange. His mother asks what most parents ask:

What do you say, Bart?

Expecting to hear the words "Thank you," he instead said: "Peel It."

How rude. How sad. How ungrateful. This is how some men feel —unappreciated.

> *Proverbs 14:1 (NLT) A wise woman builds her home, but a foolish woman tears it down with her own hands.*

Short Story for Consideration

Joe always remembers to take out the trash cans before everyone is awake. Joe ensures that he gets the mail, places it on the table for his wife, and even puts her favorite coffee on in the morning before he leaves. Joe's wife doesn't appreciate these things or even has a positive word at the end of his long day's work supporting the family. Instead, he finds himself bracing for her list of things he did wrong and feeling broken and disheartened. When a co-worker compliments him on his work ethic and his new shirts, he finds his attention turned from his wife toward that person and away from his relationship, eroding it to a place of sadness, anger, mistrust, and eventually separation.

But what is appreciation?

What does it mean to appreciate him?

To appreciate your man means

- ✓ Set a fair and unprejudiced value on him
- ✓ Respect and admire him for his full worth
- ✓ Be grateful for him
- ✓ Be thankful for all he does for you

How to Develop Appreciation for Your Man

1) The Third Eye

Learn to view him through new eyes. Women are often blinded by their familiarity and annoyances to see and appreciate a man's true value.

- Did you know that true love has three eyes?
    - The first eye is dim, dim to his faults.
    - The second eye sees him as everyone else sees him, as the world sees him.
    - The third eye sees him as no one else does or can see him. This eye appreciates him like no

one else. If you keep focusing on this eye, you will see things you never have before. You will notice many things to appreciate.

All great wives have a third eye!

2) Superficial or True Worth?

- Are you one that has focuses on your man's superficial qualities? Like his looks, his worth in money, his job, his friends. Is your ideal man one with great success and lots of money? Does he need to be a high achiever and know all the "right" people? Do you expect him to be like other men, whether in looks or wealth?
- Or you can focus on his true value. But you need to know what that true value means.
- Character: honesty, dependability, kindness, love
- Intelligence: education, knowledge, good judgment, creative skills, imagination.
- What he does for you: opens doors for you, remembers special days, doing chores, helping with children, stopping at the store.

Other things to appreciate:

- ✓ Around the house fix-it jobs
- ✓ Yardwork
- ✓ Time he spends with your children
- ✓ Things he buys for you
- ✓ His occupation
- ✓ That he has a job or is actively seeking one

- ✓ Provides home and car
- ✓ Takes care of the finances

Undervalued Men

For many years, a man's efforts have been so undervalued and less visible to women. I don't know if it's because many women are so focused on how strong women are and don't need a man for anything, or if they just forgot how to appreciate the privilege they've been given, the gift that they have, of having a companion, a life partner, a friend.

When they focus on the superficial qualities of their men, they automatically forget that he has true worth and true value. That there is so much for you to appreciate about him. It saddens my heart when I see a wife that is mean and unappreciative toward her husband. He is a human. He is a person. He does have feelings. He can be fragile. Please, please, don't break your man. He needs you.

One great failure in marriage is an ungrateful wife. The lack of appreciation toward your husbands will push them away from you to those that appreciate them. If you wonder why he never wants to be home, could it be that he has an ungrateful wife? When children see mom so ungrateful to dad, they will carry on that tradition into their lives and future marriages. I don't think this is your intention, but if you don't make a conscious effort to notice your shortcomings, then the path will be divorce and future generations that follow mom.

What if you can't find a good quality to appreciate?

Maybe it's because your heart has become so hardened, or you forgot how to use that Third Eye to see his real value.

Here are a few things you can do:

1. *Have Faith in His Worth* - Have faith that he was designed and created with kindness, intelligence, and character. Don't treat him as he is, but what his potential can be. He will become what you encourage and love him for. This doesn't mean to change him into your idea of a man and husband, but encourage his true worth, not superficial ideas.

   There may have been a long period of time when no one has had faith in him, or maybe he never had anyone believe in him. He only needs you to believe in him. He requires you to encourage him because his current life does not do justice to his true character.

2. *Visit the Past* - If you can't currently find something to appreciate him for, look into your past with him when you were dating, engaged, or newly married. Why did you fall in love with him? What qualities did you see then that you admired and couldn't live without? What things did you do together?

   He may just need to be reminded of how great things were and how you loved and appreciated him. That could be the encouragement he needs to move forward. If he's been depressed or just down, this could be the motive for living and striving.

3. *Look for Value Beneath His Faults*

Is he Obnoxious? Does he pick arguments, disagree, and take revenge on you or your marriage? Look beneath the surface. Maybe he is a high achiever that hasn't been appreciated for his full worth. This can be very frustrating to anyone and cause them to act out.

Is he Moody? Maybe he has been discouraged for many years. He may have high aspirations that haven't been met or have been made fun of or not believed in. Don't only appreciate his high goals, but his frustration for not reaching them. Encourage him to keep trying.

Is he Forgetful or Thoughtless? Does he seem to forget the things that are important to you? Maybe he doesn't think about your feelings, or it at least seems that way? He may be absorbed in things he considers more important, like keeping his job or paying the bills. Learn what is important to him and appreciate what he considers important.

Is he Negligent at Home? Does he forget to do his house chores or yard work? Does it feel like he will never get to that honey-do list? His priorities may just be different from yours. And he may be putting all of his energy into succeeding at work, to get a raise or a promotion. Learn what his priorities are, why they are and how you can appreciate them.

Think of his good side, his good values. Please, make a list of his virtues, including character, intelligence, and the things he does for you. During the week, make a conscious effort to express your appreciation for these things.

- ✓ Appreciation is gratitude
- ✓ Express your gratitude to him
- ✓ Consider his accomplishments
- ✓ Praise him in front of others
- ✓ Don't tear him down with your tongue
- ✓ When your friends hear you speak of your husband, they should note that they are words of kindness, not railing and complaining.
- ✓ Rather than sharing his weaknesses, faults, or problems, speak of him kindly, saying things that would please him to hear you say.
- ✓ Watch your tone. Please, do not speak to him as though you are talking to one of the kids. Your tone should be courteous and kind, not critical, sharp, or flippant.

Men are creatures who need response and reaction. Your verbal or nonverbal responses or reaction affirms and validate him. If he does something for you and there is no responses or reaction from you, you communicate something. For example: If he gives you flowers & there is no response or reaction, you are non verbally communicating, "Don't Do That Again!" Listen, the behavior you always reward is the behavior he will always repeat.

**Appreciate a Man's effort
Sometimes you just don't know**

**What they had to go through
just to keep you happy**

HOMEWORK

1. What are three things your man does that you appreciate? Have you told him this lately?

2. Close your eyes and think back to the last twenty-four hours. Have you said anything you can think of that might make your man feel unappreciated?

3. Have you, for one week, intentionally tried sharing with your man something you appreciate about him? Remember habits form over time, so as you give and receive this appreciation, a habit of doing so can be learned.

HOMEWORK

1. What are three things your man does that you appreciate? Have you told him this lately?

2. Close your eyes and think back to the last twenty four hours. Have you said anything you can think of that might make your man feel unappreciated?

3. Invite your man to lunch, just the two of you, and tell your man something you appreciate about him. Remember he/she isn't, offer time, so do you give and receive this appreciation, most of down so can be earned.

32

Chapter 3

Respect Says
I Will Follow Your Leadership and Submit to Your Authority

When driving a vehicle on the roads, we all know that we must stop when the lights turn red. This is an excellent example of submitting to the authority of traffic signals (red, green, and yellow lights), which keep traffic patterns in order and people safe. Ignoring the authority of said lights leads to catastrophic collisions and accidents.

> *1 Peter 3:1-2 (NLT)[1] In the same way, you wives must accept the authority of your husbands. Then, even if some refuse to obey the Good News, your godly lives will speak to them without any words. They will be won over [2] by observing your pure and reverent lives.*

Short Story for Consideration

Roger discusses the purchase of a new car with his wife. After the discussion, it is decided that this would be a luxury and unnecessary for their current situation. When Roger is at work the following day, his wife goes to the dealership and purchases the car without consulting him. Additionally, she gets defensive and angry when he asks about the decision and not submitting to their conversation. This erodes Roger's authority and weakens their relationship in ways that begin to get worse with time.

What Is Authority?

The dictionary definition of authority is the right to give orders, make decisions and enforce obedience. For instance, the authority of officials/referees in sports keeps the athletic games in order. Have you ever seen a game where officials failed to make a call, and someone got hurt? To keep the rules, orders, and compliance, someone must have the authority to decide when something is not legal in games or people can get hurt and chaos ensues.

Respect for authority[2]

Of course, this means that when two people are involved in a situation where one has the authority, the other must release their control. This is where respect comes in. One person must respect the other and trust them to make the best decisions possible. That doesn't mean that a question might not arise or even a discussion about said decision. It does mean that, in the end, a person holds the right, with all information at their disposal, to exercise the authority to decide.

Respect for HIS authority[3]

Now, in relationships, this might be where a point of contention arises. Women, you might question submitting to your man's authority and why this is important for the success of a relationship and a man feeling respected. Please, remember that in so doing, you respect Him that made us, in that God is the ultimate authority who Himself, in the Scripture, relegated said authority to the form of man.

I love the idea of middle managers when it comes to making a case for your man's authority. If you have been in a middle management decision, you are close enough to concerns to know what should be done based on experience. You can plead a case to upper management (ultimate authority figures) and even lay out a course of action. In the end, though, we have all been on the receiving end of a decision that did not fully align with our opinions. If you left a company or rebelled by doing something harmful every time this happened – you wouldn't have a job for long. Rather, you learn to respect authority and abide by the authority of those higher on the organizational chart than yourself. So, this should also be understood in any relationship.

Wive's submission[4] [5]

Wive's submission to their husband is an act of trust. Trust in your husband, and trust in God who ordained the authority in your husband. It is easy to do this when things are great and decisions are easy or effortless. It will be more difficult in struggle, relationship strain, or even hard choices where you do not align with the outcome. It is critical to remain communicative, open to discussions, and feel cherished to share your opinion. When done, as the final authority, you must lie at the feet of your husband as God instructed and show him the respect to flex that authority in the manner he sees fit.

Remember, submission is not obeying. A husband should not do anything illegal, immoral, or harmful to his wife to be allocated the authority by his wife. Additionally, this is not dictating all aspects of the home as you would good behavior to a child. Rather, wives are partners and helpmates for their husbands and should be treated as such. Authority in this context is just the final upper manager in the relationship, who should hold the authority of the final decision. Respect, communication, and love will help smooth the path to this authority being freely given from a place of trust and respect on the part of a wife.

Why might a man not exercise his authority?

- ✓ Frustration, as he was not shown respect or trust to use his authority in the past.
- ✓ Inappropriate behavior toward him in the past, when he exercised authority.
- ✓ Threats made about what would happen should he make a decision.

How to show your respect for his authority:

- ✓ Express disagreements privately
- ✓ Praise him when he makes good decisions
- ✓ Lift in prayer for the heavyweight of decisions he bears
- ✓ Gracious when you don't agree with his decisions
- ✓ Do not try manipulating the decision; this never works as intended.

HOMEWORK

1. Think about the last time your man exercised his authority? How did you react? Do you think you should have reacted differently?

2. Do you respect your man's authority? We know this is a tough question, and you don't have to tell anyone, just meditate on that and the truth in your heart for a moment.

3. What two things do you think could help you in respecting your man's authority? Can you discuss these with him?

Chapter 4

Respect Says

I Will Show You Attention & Meet Your Sexual Needs

Remember the billboard topping hit by Tina Turner, "*What's Love Got to Do With It?*" The words were a bit of a departure from most love songs:

> *You must understand though the touch of your hand*
> *Makes my pulse react*
> *That it's only the thrill of boy meeting girl*
> *Opposites attract*
> *It's physical*
> *Only logical*
> *You must try to ignore that it means more than that*
>
> *What's love got to do, got to do with it?*
> *What's love but a second-hand emotion?*
> *What's love got to do, got to do with it?*
> *Who needs a heart when a heart can be broken?*

Sexual fulfillment is necessary as a one-time event or ongoing component of a relationship. Respect for your man will ensure that these, like other needs, are met to ensure love does have something to do with the sexual side of your relationship, as Tina might not have understood what sex, love, and a strong relationship had to do with each other, but God most certainly did.

1 Corinthians 7:1-2 (NIV) [1] Now for the matters you wrote about: "It is good for a man not to have sexual relations with a woman." [2] But since sexual immorality is occurring, each man should have sexual relations with his own wife, and each woman with her own husband.

Short Story for Consideration

Steve had been married to Shondra for six months now. At first, she would take extra care for their dates to dress nicely and smell heavenly. Their courtship and eventual marriage were a mixture of amazing conversations, shared goals, and her always making him feel special with her care taken in dressing for his business dinners. Last night, though, he had arrived to pick her up for the company picnic, and she looked as if she pulled the outfit from the hamper. In her defense, she said she had a long day, and she knew all these people and didn't know why she needed to make an effort. Today, he is still thinking and feels as if she didn't bother even making the smallest efforts for him, either. Of course, when they got home from the night out, she went straight to bed, and he had to go without what he was hoping would be the highlight of the evening for both of them.

Sexual Needs Are Important

The sexual attraction might be considered by some an event that should never involve the heart, just as Tina sang about. Or, in some cases, that initial spark that fizzles with the more time you spend with a person. Not so in a solid relationship with your man. Men crave a sexual environment where you always make them feel sexy, care for, and most of all, attractive. Respect for your man and his needs means putting in the effort to remain attractive to him and show him that only he can fulfill those needs for you. Most importantly, you want to be the one taking care of all your sexual needs to build intimacy and strength into the relationship.

He needs sexual fulfillment[6]

This is not a wish list item for a man, but sexual fulfillment is a need. Sexual fulfillment predates your relationship, of course, and so knowing what your man requires in this area is critical for a respectful, nurturing relationship. Assuming this will wane or disappear after marriage or an extended time together is a falsehood. Sure, age and health concerns will sometimes cause men's sexual needs to peak or dip. At all times, though, respect for your man includes meeting those needs.

The Scripture about the needs of man is well known by the God that created him. He has dictated that a man take one wife and be faithful while still understanding the needs they need to meet. As a respectful partner to your man, ensuring you understand this component of your relationship will be critical to the health and longevity of your time together.

He is not a monster; he is a man![7]

Communication is critical for you to be able to meet your man's sexual needs. Men give easy-to-read queues and if the timing, frequency, or urgency are making you uncomfortable, talk about it, don't just withhold or passively find ways to turn him off.

What is your favorite food on earth? Now imagine that your man is holding that food up and over your head. You can see it, smell it and imagine what it is going to taste like. And then, without warning, he tosses it in the trash and walks away. How would you feel?

Your man desires you and wants to respect and remain faithful to you alone. He is dressing as he likes, wearing that favorite perfume, and sitting just close enough to make him imagine all kinds of fantasies with you as the star. And then you suddenly walk to bed, and put on the fuzzy pajamas, and go to bed. When he reaches for you, slapping his hand away, you tell him no. How do you suppose he feels now? Is that loving, respectful, or in any way conducive to a happy, productive relationship? Of course not; keeping your man happy and satiated is essential to your relationship. It will help if you put as much work into this aspect as to the authority you relegate, respect, and admiration you show him.

Show Him You Respect His Needs

When we start dating, getting to know people's discussions of sex might be a tough conversation to start. As time progresses and the relationship deepens, we talk about children, future hopes, and admirations – and we definitely should be talking about our sexual fulfillment requirements. Discuss where you are and what you require, and give him a platform to do the same.

Have you heard Rihanna's song Unfaithful? Boy, did she hit the nail on the head with that one! Listen, Infidelity among a man or woman is not always about sex. I've counseled couples that it isn't really about whom you lie with; it's whom you lie to. To prevent unfaithfulness, always talk about what you specifically need from each other how you can meet those needs. If you don't meet your partner's needs, somebody else just might.

As time goes, continue to show your man respect by dressing to please him and even tease him on occasion. Your clothes, perfume, and playful touches are not emotional tools to hold him hostage when you need something. They should serve to continue to bind you together in meaningful ways. The sexual fulfillment should, in time, come from the heart and deep abiding respect to continue to honor your man and his commitment to you alone.

How to Respectfully Meet His Sexual Needs

- ✓ Surprise him and keep it fresh
- ✓ Know what he requires and meet those needs
- ✓ Men are visual, so be creative
- ✓ Discuss what each of your need

HOMEWORK

1. Do you feel you are showing respect by meeting all your man's sexual fulfillment needs? How do you know you are/are not? Have you talked about this?

2. What is the one thing you might try to do more, less, or differently to enhance this aspect of your relationship? If we asked your man, would his answer be the same?

3. When first dating, and now – is your sexual fulfillment with your partner more or less what you had hoped for? Would your man answer the same? Why or why not?

Chapter 5

Respect Says
I Will Be Available and Play With You

There was a study done starting in 1996[8] in Denver, Colorado, with 306 couples. The study has been featured on the news and other sites and books, as it proved the statement that couples that play together stay together. This study and others have shown that actual fun activities, not just alone time, build the healthiest of relationships. One of the reasons couples have trouble is that they have different takes on fun and bonding, Parrott says. *"Intimacy and friendship for a man is built on shared activity, but for women, shared activity is a backdrop for a great conversation. What she wants on date night is a time of intimacy and friendship. He's disappointed because she'll never go to a game or golfing, and it's during shared activities that his spirit is most likely to open up."*

Short Story for Consideration

Troy has always loved dancing and has recommended many times over the years with Gina they take a class together. She has had an excuse every time. In hopes of changing her mind, he booked a wine and painting class that she wanted to do. Then a few weeks later, he even did two Saturday morning yoga sessions. They walked to the park each Saturday, got coffee, and he truly enjoyed trying something different.

Tonight, after work, he brought a flyer home for a One Day Only Salsa Class at the community center close to them. He was so excited, but when he asked her to do this with him, she got angry and told him to quit trying to pressure her into things she wouldn't enjoy. He doubts he will try again and worries that they will never find something they can enjoy if she won't try anything outside her comfort zone anymore.

He needs her availability[9]

Yes, our lives are full of work, kids, commitments, and little time for the things we might wish to do. That is no excuse for you not to take the time to be available to your man. He needs the time; while we might crave conversation and intimacy, men thrive off of time spent together in doing. What is it that he loves to do? If you aren't sure, the first step is to ask him. If you have been with your man for some length of time, you know this already. So, ask yourself why aren't you taking the time to be available to him.

Sure, jobs are important, and kids can't always do for themselves, but your relationship will never thrive if you don't show the respect your man needs by making yourself available. This is not meant for sexual fulfillment alone, but rather a time for him. Time to talk, engage, and most of all have fun doing activities that he enjoys. Why him alone? The best-case scenario won't be him alone that derives enjoyment from the activity; you both should find it beneficial and fulfilling. Instead of bringing out the excuses of being tired, exhausted, have more work, and the like – the next time your man asks about doing something together, find the time. Or better yet, surprise him and plan something for the two of you to do together he would love and show him how much you also wish to be available.

Become his recreational companion[10]

Your husband needs a playmate. A playmate is a recreational companion. While he needs male friends, YOU must become the one he can have the most fun with. Remember how you spent so much time with him when you were dating? It is very interesting that among the five basic male needs, spending recreational time with his wife is second only to sex.

Watch someone doing something they love. The golfer swinging a club on a gloriously perfect day. A boater out on the water. A sports fanatic at a game. Look at their faces and how excited they are to be in that moment. Normally, you will see them turn to the person next to them and want to share their joy at the moment. You need to be the one sitting next to your man, in that instance.

Recreational activities are reaffirming for men. They are the reason they work so hard to afford them, take time from other things to do them, and most of all might wish to share them with you. Whether just out on a boat, hiking a trail, hitting balls, or a myriad of other activities, you need to be the recreational companion for your man. Instead of allowing him to go off with buddies or himself to undertake his hobbies, offer up new alternatives or go along with him. Remember, play together, stay together, as these moments build memories, companionship, and respect by your man that you want to make time for the two of you together.

Ways to Be a Recreational Companion

- ✓ Take regular walks together
- ✓ Take day trips to new places
- ✓ Take a class together
- ✓ Join a recreational sports league
- ✓ Schedule regular "date" nights

HOMEWORK

1. What activities do you enjoy doing with your man? Are they things you are both good at, or do you do them begrudgingly?

2. What activity have you always thought would be amazing to learn and aren't yet proficient at? Is this something your man would/could do with you? Have you asked him to try this new activity?

3. Think about this past week and divide all your activities into buckets (i.e., work, errands, sleep). Now, what percentage did you do together with your man? How many prevented you from being available to him or things you could do together? Are there changes, maybe, that need to be made here?

Chapter 6

Respect Says

I Will Keep Myself Attractive and Work on My Inner/Outer Beauty

The Big Bang Theory was a show that was about scientists, with a twist (or maybe a tad more than that) of humor. In one scene later in the series, dating couple, Penny and Leonard went to one of Leonard's University meetings where he was vying for a promotion. Most of the members of the committee that would be deciding his fate were men, and thus he had Penny dress skimpily with her chest on full display. Even Leonard's friends were transfixed, and it made for some good laughs. It also provided something science already knows, men are visually stimulated, whereas women tend to find more connections via communication, gestures, and such.

1 John 2:16 (NIV) For everything in the world-the lust of the flesh, the lust of the eyes, and the pride of life—comes not from the Father but the world.

God knew the lust of the things seen could take humans off course. To this end, you need to be the source of attraction that your man wishes to lust after and stay faithful. This requires you to be respectful in your attentiveness to your looks and draw his eyes always to you.

Short Story for Consideration

Stanley could remember that first time he saw Jane. She had walked in wearing this bright red lipstick that matched the dress that clung to every curve. He had to talk to her, and they spent the entire night and every day since together. To reconnect after so many years of marriage, he asked that they start a weekly date night. Tonight is the first one, and he has taken time to get fresh flowers, shower, put on his best pants and dress shirt. Then he allowed her time to prepare as he waited with bated breath downstairs. He couldn't wait, and when he finally heard the footsteps coming in his direction, his breath caught in his chest. Turning, his stomach plummeted when he found her wearing just some jeans and a shirt that he had seen her in a million times.

"I thought we agreed to get dressed up," he said, trying to hide the hurt.

"Come on, Stanley," she said, waving absently at him. "I just want to be comfortable after all these years. Did you need to see me in some sexy dress with this extra weight I've put on?"

"Baby, you always look good to me," he said, moving in close, trying to sugar her up.

"Come on now, you know I have pottery class in the morning," she complained. "I need something quick and early to bed for me after the week I've had."

Stanley almost told her they could just grab something at home as disappointed as he was. He didn't bother giving her the flowers and later that night found himself staring at the ceiling for a long time, wondering if everything was simply downhill from here.

Men are VISUAL. Women Are Verbal.

"Research found that men tend to use one side of their brain (particularly the left side for verbal reasoning) while women tend to use both cerebral areas for visual, verbal, and emotional responses. These differences in brain use cause a difference in behavior between men and women. Women tend to be better at sensing emotional messages in conversations, gestures, and facial expressions and are thus more sensitive. Women start to speak and read at an earlier age than men and are generally better in verbal skills, such as learning a different language. They tend to grasp grammar and spelling better, and girls have better handwriting than boys do. Women have better sight at night and have a more acute sense of smell, taste, and hearing."

This means that just because you love some great conversations and feel closer to your man after – that he will feel the same. Sweat pants might be the most comfortable driving kids around, but they don't elicit a man to stare. You might not care that you didn't do your hair for two days because the kids had full soccer practice; he does. You feel tired, so don't care what you look like, and your man had nothing pretty to gaze at. It is easy enough to put on something comfortable and attractive for him at the end of a long day. When picking out clothes that work for your lifestyle, can they also enhance whatever part of your anatomy he likes?

You have a few extra pounds after baby one and two, but he loves that new backside. So, give him a full view in some soft and comfortable yoga pants that make running around easy but will make him mad in the head when you bend over to take the dishes from the dishwasher later. Maybe throwing your hair up is easier for you, but that sexy librarian look when you shake it out in front of him might just win you bonus points and his devotion at the end of a long day.

Men are visual, so respectfully find a way to play up those assets to remind him, constantly, why he first found you attractive. Don't give his eyes any chance to look someplace else. You know what he likes the best, and with just a tiny bit of effort, you can show him you care by playing those up for his eyes alone.

He needs an attractive spouse[11]

When you meet someone for the first time, their looks matter; you don't walk up to a smelly, unclean person in the bar and strike up a conversation. If we are honest, men and women will seek out the most aesthetically pleasing person to them at that moment. Men, being more visual, find that this is critical to their staying power in a relationship. Women tend to be the ones that allow things to go as the relationship deepens and don't see the need to still be attractive or take time to even worry about that.

Let's go back to the research. Women do this because the intimacy, conversation, and other moments with their men keep them happy. Men remain visual! This means they need you to keep with it and respect them by being the attractive partner they wish to come home to every night.

No, that doesn't mean beauty queen only needs to apply. That means that the same assets that drew him in to start, you still have it – so flaunt it. Put in the time to make those little extra efforts that remind him you care and keep his eyes glued to you. Even if sexual fulfillment, due to a host of reasons, might not be on the agenda at that moment, staying attractive, attentive to how you look, and present yourself keeps him coming back time and again.

Inner/Outer Beauty

Sure, we have talked about the visual aspects of beauty, but inner beauty shows through just as much. Learning new things, volunteering to help others genuinely, and advocating for a cause you believe in also have merit. When you are helping expand your inner beauty in different ways, your man will take notice. You act more confident, engage him in conversations about your day and glow with contagious happiness at home. While doing the little things outwardly to keep your man engaged is critical to your relationship, do not underestimate how much an inner beauty will impact this aspect of your relationship, as well.

How to Be More Attractive for Him

- ✓ Stand up straight
- ✓ Try a new scent you think he would like
- ✓ A new nightgown (throw the flannel out)
- ✓ Just a few pounds off, you feel better, and he will take notice
- ✓ Good hygiene, even if you have nowhere to be
- ✓ Volunteer together for a cause

HOMEWORK

1. What do you think about dressing for your man? What are two little things you do just because you know he likes them?

2. Is there anything you think you could do for the man that would cause him not to take his eyes off you? How can you tell when your man is enjoying something you are doing?

3. Name something you did when you were newly dating to attract your man, that you don't do anymore? Why? Name one thing you could do now that you couldn't do when you were first dating that your man would appreciate?

Chapter 7

Respect Says

I will Attend to You and Serve you

Let me cater to you song by Destiny's Child explains what domestic support looks like:

Baby I see you working hard

Wanna let you know I'm proud

Let you know that I admire what you do

Don't know if I need to reassure you

My life would be purposeless without you (yeah)

If I want it (you got it)

When I ask you (you provide it)

You inspire me to be better

You challenge me for the better

Sit back and let me pour out my love letter

Let me help you

Take off your shoes

Untie your shoestrings

Take off your cuff-links (yeah)

What you wanna eat boo? (yeah)

Let me feed you

Let me run your bathwater

Whatever you desire

I'll supply ya

Sing you a song

Turn the game on

I'll brush your hair

Help you put your do-rag on

Want a foot rub? (yeah)

Want a manicure?

Baby I'm yours

I wanna cater to you boy

Let me cater to you

'Cause baby this is your day

Do anything for my man

Baby you blow me away

I got your slippers, your dinner, your dessert, and so much more

Anything you want

Just let me cater to you

Inspire me from the heart

Can't nothing tear us apart

You're all I want in a man

  I put my life in your hands

I got your slippers, your dinner, your dessert, and so much more

Anything you want

Genesis 2:18 (NIV) The LORD God said, "It is not good for the man to be alone. I will make a helper suitable for him."

The translation for helper or helpmate in the Scripture is one to help him in all the affairs of life, not only for the propagation of his species, but to provide things useful and comfortable for him; to dress his food, and take care of the affairs of the family; one "like himself."[12]

Short Story for Consideration

Tim works hard each day as a financial advisor. After a twelve-hour day at the office, he comes home to find that Reena has once again not done laundry, no food waiting, and she is actually on the couch with a glass of wine talking to a girlfriend. When he asks for dinner, she snaps that he doesn't understand what it is like being home with a one-year-old all day. She asks for him to take care of himself, as he is a big boy, while she unwinds with a friend for just a few moments. He wanders to the kitchen and can't even find a clean pan in which to fry a steak; sad and so tired, he grabs a drink and just walks down to his man cave to watch television. He finds himself responding to his administrative assistant when she asks about getting him lunch or other tiny favors. He no longer understands why he bothers to work this hard for a wife that takes him for granted in such a way.

He needs domestic support[13]

This should be a conversation early in a relationship about how you see the break out of domestic chores. In this day and age, more and more men and women hold staunch views on dishes, laundry, yard work, caring for children, and anything else that goes into managing a household.

In ages gone past, with men as the breadwinner and women at home, this distinction was much clearer. These days, even men will state that they can do more for themselves, as many live independently for years before marriage. However, men need domestic support as careers blossom, kids arrive, and more responsibilities play out in the home. Knowing where those lines are before they explode into resentment, anger, and unhappy relationships is critical.

What does he need for Domestic Support?"

- ✓ Who should do dishes and such daily?
- ✓ Who does the lawn work?
- ✓ Whose hours at a secular job outweigh the other?
- ✓ How much stress does an unclean home put on a man?
- ✓ How has chores in the home divided your man's family?

Disparities in the running of your home should be early conversations, as these are some of the largest disagreements in marriage. Knowing expectations and being able to meet them based on your needs, upbringing, and understanding of biblical truths in your home is critical. Like so many topics that should be discussed earlier in a relationship, this topic must be addressed. Sure, times have changed, but assuming you know what that will mean for you and your man, you will know it's not a good idea. Clean and clear guidelines upfront will ensure smooth sailing as life gets complicated and busier down the road.

HOMEWORK

1. How are the household chores split currently? Do you split them 50/50 or do you expect your man to do more than that? How often do you complain about everything on your plate to get done?

2. Is there anything that your man does unsolicited by you that you truly appreciate? What about you, two things you do to ease his burden without even expecting recognition?

3. How often do you argue about who should do something within the home? Why do you feel it needs to be equally split? What would happen if you did more of the domestic support without a scoreboard?

Chapter 8

Respect Says

I Will Acknowledge Your Language of Love

When talking about Love Languages, Kehlani's song by the same name gives insights into how to approach this important aspect of your relationship:

> *A lot of ways to love you*
> *Teach me through your eyes*
> *What is needed for you*
> *Needed in your life*
> *Don't wanna go shopping*
> *You want picnics in the park*
> *Do you like mornings*
> *Should we do it in the dark*
> *It's all foreign to me, I don't speak what you speak*
> *I'll commit to learning if you, if you*
> *You're a sweet fantasy, singing your ABC's*
> *Please be patient with me, will you*
> *Said I wanna be fluent in your love language*
> *Learning your love language*
> *I know I don't speak your language*

But I wanna know more, baby

Fluent in your love language

Learning your love language

I know I don't speak your language

But I wanna know more, baby

Never wanna get lost in translation

Never wanna be on two separate pages

Swear to me that you'll state facts

If you can take back, know I can take that

I been working at it, hoping that you'd notice

I been waiting, I just needed you to focus

Swear to me that you'll show me

Need you to coach me, then we can proceed

Short Story for Consideration

Neal's love language is words of affirmation. He had been formulating a poem for days that he felt would tell her how much their time together mattered to him, and he adored her. When he bent and spoke the words he had been contemplating on all day, she just stared at him absently. When he was finished, she gazed at him hurt. "This is our anniversary, and all you got me was a few lousy words of poetry?" She spat out as she rose from the couch and ran from the room. The following day, she sent him a text that she had thought this was important to him and that she had spent a lot of money on his gift, a replica of his grandfather's watch he had in the war. She didn't understand him believing some sweet words to her was enough, and she couldn't be with someone so cheap. That relationship ended, but she came across information on love languages one day and finally understood the disconnect.

Love Languages (Taco Style)[14]

Gary Chapman, years ago, talked about five ways humans best receive love from others. It is critical to understand these, as you and your man might not have the same love language, and acknowledging this early allows you to accommodate his love language and shapes how you communicate your love for him. Additionally, understanding the language you speak in is important because if your man's language is different, it could cause disconnects in his understanding of what you are speaking.

- **Words of Affirmation** - Saying supportive things to your partner.
    - **As applied to tacos**: Your tacos are delicious.
- **Acts of Service** - Doing helpful things for your partner.
    - **As applied to tacos**: I made you tacos.
- **Receiving Gifts** - Giving your partner gifts that tell them you were thinking about them.
    - **As applied to tacos**: Here's a Taco.
- **Quality Time** - Spending meaningful time with your partner.
    - **As applied to tacos**: Let's go out for tacos together.

- **Physical Touch** - Being close to and caressed by your partner.
    - As **applied to tacos**: Let me hold you like at taco.

HOMEWORK

1. Do you know your love language? What about your man's?

2. What is something you do to let your man know you acknowledge his love language? What has his response been to this action?

3. If your love languages are not the same, what ways have you both found to acknowledge and validate the language of the other?

Conclusion

You Make Him Better!

Make Me Better[15] is the third single from Fabolous's album, *From Nothin' to Somethin'*. The song features Ne-Yo on the hook and is produced by Timbaland.

[Chorus: Ne-Yo]

I'm a movement by myself (Oh!)

But I'm a force when we're together

Mami, I'm good all by myself (Oh!)

But baby you, you make me better

You make me better, You make me better (Hey! Hey!)

You make me better, You make me better (Hey! Hey!)

You make me better, You make me better (Hey! Hey!)

You make me better, You make me better (Hey! Hey! Hey!)

[Verse 1: Fabolous]

You plus me, it equals better math

Your boy a good look but she my better half

I'm already bossin, already flossin

But why have the cake if it ain't got the sweet frostin

You're-You're-You're-You're keepin me on my A-game

With-With-With-Without havin the same name

They-They-They-They-They-They might flame

But-But-But-But shorty we burn it up

The sag and my swag, pep in my step

Daddy do the Gucci mami in Giuseppes

Guess it's a G thing whenever we swing

I'm a need Coretta Scott if I'm 'gon be King (Oooh)

Your man might be a force by himself, as the song says, but together you are that much better. Appreciate him, be a helpmate to him, fulfill him sexually and acknowledge his love language are just some of the ways you will make your relationship go the long run.

HelpMate

Meriam Webster[16] says a helpmate is a companion and helper, especially: wife. You can be your man's helpmate in all things and together build the relationship both of you can be proud of and stand as examples to others. If you admire him, show him how you appreciate him by respectfully submitting to his authority. You are well on your way on this by making yourself his recreational companion to play together while maintaining your attractiveness inside and out to more fully fulfill his sexual attention. Finally, as a helpmate carrying the domestic load, communicating all needs, and acknowledging the love language, he speaks for the best results.

You can be the companion to walk alongside your man in unity and togetherness by completing him.

Complete Him

Like two halves of a whole, neither your man nor you will feel complete without the other. Remember, this is a partnership where both bring to the relationship their roles, responsibilities, and a cohesive spirit of putting you aside to better the whole. This is not a competition or a race to see who can be the superior in your relationship, as the Bible has already allocated this to your man.

When a mother Eagle builds a nest for her young, she uses thorns, thistles, jagged stones, and other sharp objects as the nest's infrastructure? Why? Because if she makes the nest "too comfortable," her babies will never leave the nest & soar above the clouds. Ladies, that's why things sometimes are so uncomfortable and miserable for you in your relationship! Could it be that our heavenly Father is trying to get you out of your "comfort zone?" Could it be that He wants to take you higher this year! In my R Kelley voice - I Believe I Can Fly!

You must find it within yourself to follow the dictates of the Scripture on this, which science continues to prove out. Neither man nor woman is better; a man without a woman is missing a vital part of themselves. Man-nerisms help you understand how best to execute your piece of this relationship, and the next book will show them how best to treat you in return. Together you will walk as God intended and reap the benefits of a respectful and fulfilling relationship.

References

[1] https://www.marriagebuilders.com/admiration.htm

[2] https://tonyevans.org/seeing-the-secret/

[3] https://www.crystalstorms.me/2014/05/love-respect-desire-authority/

[4] https://www.gty.org/library/bibleqnas-library/QA0022/wives-marriage-and-submission

[5] https://www.gty.org/library/sermons-library/80-382/the-willful-submission-of-a-christian-wife

[6] https://www.marriagebuilders.com/sexual-fulfillment.htm

[7] https://marriagemissions.com/husbands-sexual-needs-man-monster/

[8] https://abcnews.go.com/Health/Family/story?id=5387217&page=1

[9] https://www.marriagebuilders.com/recreational-companionship.htm

[10] https://www.marriageandfamilytoday.com/husbands-recreational-companion/

[11] https://www.marriagebuilders.com/physical-attractiveness.htm

[12] https://www.biblestudytools.com/genesis/2-18.html

[13] https://www.marriagebuilders.com/domestic-support.htm

[14] https://www.psychologytoday.com/intl/blog/click-here-happiness/202009/what-are-the-5-love-languages-definition-and-examples

[15] Lyrics: https://genius.com/Fabolous-make-me-better-lyrics

[16] https://www.merriam-webster.com/dictionary/helpmate

Do you need RELATIONSHIP HELP?

Shawn McBride offers virtual counseling to clients all over the world.

Are you struggling in your dating, engaged or marriage relationship with:

1. Infidelity, trust issues, recovering from betrayal/affair?
2. Difficulty communicating or resolving conflict?
3. Feeling emotionally disconnected from your partner?
4. Talking in circles with your partner?
5. Feeling stuck & having the same fights over and over again?
6. Feelings of anger, bitterness & resentment?
7. Feeling unheard & misunderstood by your partner?
8. Not feeling appreciated/lack affection in the relationship?

We specialize in working with couples in the most difficult situations. Let us walk with you on your relationship journey and help you:

1. Work through the tough relational issues that you are facing.
2. Teach you and your partner new relational skills.
3. Teach you proven relational tools.
4. Guide you to create the kind of relationship that THRIVES!

No matter where you find yourself in your relationship, we will always listen to your story and professionally assess your relationship at the Couples Counseling Center. With our professional help, you can replace frustration, anger, and worry with deeper understanding, affirmation, and fulfillment in your relationship.

Schedule your appointment with us today and get the professional assistance you need for your relationship!

www.CouplesCounselingCenter.org

Shawn McBride Teaching Resources

Mindset Reset – ISBN: 978-1092500227
Mindset Reset is a practical book that will teach readers eight core principles of mindset renewal that will significantly enhance their lives.

Handling Life's Struggles – ISBN: 978-1986754071
This 31-day devotional will inform, inspire and impact the lives of every reader who is currently facing any life adversity.

The Power of Words – ISBN: 978-1514330388
Readers will discover the importance and necessity of speaking positive words of affirmation into young people's lives and will find the dangers and ramifications of speaking words of death.

Beware of Bad Company – ISBN: 978-1484850039
Beware of Bad Company is an eye-opening and practical book for people of all ages. It offers vibrant, sensible teaching on the importance of evaluating relationships.

How to Become a Successful Student – ISBN: 978-1505437607
American children spend at least 16-20 years of their lives receiving formal education. How To Become a Successful Student enlightens young people with 26 practical and easy-to-remember principles from A-Z that will help them excel in this journey.

Know Your Worth – ISBN 978-1495453939
Know Your Worth is an empowering & inspirational 365-day devotional book written to help teenage girls grow in wisdom and understanding about issues relevant to their stage in life.

The 5 Needs of Every Teenager – ISBN 978-1548093532
Far too many young people today feel disconnected, ignored, and completely alienated from parents and adults alike. After 25 years of working with adolescents, McBride wrote this important book to enlighten parents and caring adults on what teenagers need relationally and emotionally to connect with them.

Shawn McBride's 52 Object Lessons – ISBN 978-1088489000
> This book teaches you to harness the power of object lessons for those who follow you, whether they be your children, the children of others, or adults longing to know and understand the Lord.

The 5 Steps to Achieve Your Big, Hairy, and Audacious Goals – ISBN 979-8656384407
> This book will inspire, challenge, and teach anyone who has the inner desire and internal ambition to go hard after their BIG GOALS, BIG DREAMS, and BIG DESIRES!

40 Days with Jesus! – ISBN: 979-8640215441
> 40 Days With Jesus was written to help Christians form the habit of daily devotion learning from our Lord & Savior. Because the words of Jesus are life-changing and timeless, the 40 daily lessons only focus on the words that he spoke.

All materials on sale on Amazon in paperback and Kindle versions.

Or visit:

https://truthforyouth-417873.square.site/